the MIND
of CHRIST

Impacting Lives, Transforming Minds

the MIND
of CHRIST

Impacting Lives, Transforming Minds

Michael A. Roberson, Jr.

Printed in the United States of America
Keen Vision Publishing, LLC
www.publishwithKVP.com
ISBN: 978-1-948270-89-2

For Carter and Christian, whom I love dearly. Thank you for continually providing me incentive to be an example of embracing and developing the mind of Christ.

For all individuals who desire to live a life holy and acceptable unto God.

table of CONTENTS

foreword

The *Mind of Christ* publication is a must-have. Not only is Michael my spiritual son, he is one of my brightest pupils. While serving as his mentor, I have witnessed Michael work tirelessly to mentally record and recall many of the core values that are vital to believers. Among them, having the mind of Christ has always been a supreme priority.

I truly believe that as a man thinketh in his heart, so is he. What we harvest and harbor in the mind is important. The words that come out of our mouths are usually based on the information retained in our minds. In this publication, Michael does a great job of leading the reader into correct perspectives for various seasons of life. You will find new reasons to conform to the image of Jesus Christ while progressing to the likeness of his mind. This alone will provide you with the ability to reason with God rather than continuously questioning him. Through Michael's writing, you will be challenged to face the issues lurking in the corridors of your heart. I strongly recommend this book. Congratulations, Michael, on a job well done!

Metropolitan Archbishop Lorenzo N. Peterson

introduction

Everything we do and every action we commit originates in our minds. Yes, all of our conscious and unconscious habits began in our minds first. If we are going to be victorious and sanctified in our ways of living, we must adjust our paradigm and perspective and walk in the mind of Christ. As we embrace the mindset of Jesus Christ, we welcome the mindset of God's Kingdom. If we refuse to embrace the mindset of Christ, the Kingdom of God cannot actively penetrate the earth. I desire that through this book, you will begin to understand and embrace Christ's way of thinking, as this is the only way you can portray the true fruit of Jesus Christ.

Having the mind of Christ means submitting to Christ as Lord and allowing the Holy Spirit to take complete control. As we submit to Christ as Master of our lives, we declare that Christ rules us. We relinquish control over our thinking, language, and behaviors. In essence, we surrender our total identity to the Lord. In return, he teaches us how to look and behave as he does. As we learn how to live godly lives, we take on a new nature that empowers us to become partakers in the divine nature of God. We will begin to discern the spiritual things that the natural man cannot comprehend. Since our battle is not with flesh but things in the spirit, believers must have this level of discernment.

When we first give our lives to Christ, we are full of zeal to follow Christ and receive all that we can from Him. I remember the moment when I first believed. My earnest prayers were that God would reveal himself to me in a way that He had never shown to any man. I desired a unique experience with God, one that I could call my own. Nearly a decade after praying this prayer, God did reveal something to me: ME. To show me a new dimension of himself, he had to first reveal the areas of my life that didn't align with who he said I was. While living in Alaska, I had to acknowledge the generational curses that had traveled through my bloodline and attached themselves to me, such as anger and lust. Although I knew God loved me, and I loved God, I still found myself falling prey to these two spirits specifically. It was at that time when the Lord showed and began to minister to me Philippians 2:5, "Let this mind be in you which was also in Christ Jesus."

As I began my exploration of the mind of Christ, my mind began to change, my identity changed, and I became new. I am no longer who I was before God transformed my mind. The saying is true, "A changed mind is the most powerful tool anyone can receive."

By the guidance of the Holy Spirit, I wrote this book

so that others can also experience the victory of having a changed mind. If you are wondering if your mind needs transforming, look no further than your daily actions. Our actions always indicate what is in our hearts. Suppose an individual finds themselves harboring hatred and wrath, participating in rebellion against leadership or authorities, committing false testimonies, indulging in adultery, fornication, etc.? In that case, they are indeed in need of a better understanding of the mind of Christ. These acts display that our hearts require a transformation that only comes from Christ.

Thinking like Christ is a daily strive. Yes, it will take some work, but you can have the Mind of Christ. God is constantly purging our minds of the ill thoughts the world bombards us with. All we need to do is position ourselves daily to obey, sacrifice, and submit to the Lord's ways. It is like in Mark 8:28, where Jesus says, "Whosoever will come after me, let him deny himself and take up his cross daily, and follow me." Obtaining the mind of Christ is a sacrificial commitment. Paul mentions this sacrificial commitment in 1 Corinthians 15:31 as he says, "I die daily." God desires to perfect our minds; our minds' perfection requires us to reside in a posture of obedience, sacrifice, and submission daily.

You don't have to take this journey alone. Along with the help of the Lord, this book will empower and challenge you to pursue the image of Jesus Christ while chasing after His mind. Although written to empower believers, if you are an unbeliever in pursuit of understanding who Jesus Christ is, this book is for you as well.

After you read this book, I pray that your life is impacted

in several ways.

I pray you will understand the power of a mind submitted to Christ. Before your life can produce any lasting fruit, you must first change the way you think.

I pray this book impacts how you handle relationships. As you grow deeper in your understanding of the mind that Christ desires you to have, your actions, reactions and responses will change in relation to how you handle your relationships. Love, goodness, peace, patience, self-control, kindness, gentleness are factors that become a priority in our relationships when we adopt the mind of Christ.

I pray this book helps you change your life. As we truly conform to the mind of Christ, his mind becomes our natural way of thinking. Romans 7:25 teaches us that it is through the mind that we serve the Lord. As we submit to this process, the traits that we gain from the fruit of the Spirit become what we live by and implement in our everyday lives. It is vital to understand that we are and become what we are constantly thinking about. The transforming of your mind transforms your life.

I pray this book deepens your relationship with God. God desires that you mature and develop the characteristics of Jesus Christ by living a life of love and humility. The only way to grow deeper with Jesus is to submit to His mind. Growth is not automatic. To grow in the mind of Christ, you must first want to grow, decide to grow, make a consistent effort to grow, and then be determined to grow in His mind.

I pray this book helps you experience wealth in

your finances and success in your career. Scripture teaches us that the Lord desires that we may prosper and be in health, even as our soul prospers. The Lord wants us to be successful and bear good fruit in every area of our lives. Our relationship with God and our thinking play a major role in our prosperity. Many religious individuals would have you believe that God is only focused on the spiritual aspect of a man — not so. The Lord wants you to be successful in the natural as well. I am a strong believer that if we acknowledge God in all of our ways that he will direct our paths. Yes, this also applies to our finances. As we surrender our minds over unto the Lord, He gives us ideas, strategies, and instructions on what to do with our finances. I've learned from personal experiences that if we were to listen to God with our finances and the instructions that He gives, He would teach us how to earn, save, and invest money.

I pray this book leads you to embrace your purpose. If you find a mind that is aware of its purpose, you'll find a mind driven by conviction. Conviction is motivated by vision, and without vision, there is no passion. If an individual has no vision, he will walk around aimlessly. I pray that through understanding Christ's mind, you will be motivated to fulfill the purpose God has for you.

God plans to prosper you and give you a hope and a future. You won't be able to perceive the things God has in store for your life if you don't change your mind. Again, a changed mind leads to a changed life. The transformation you need will be found in your willingness to learn, trust, and obey the Lord. When you are ready to explore the Mind of Christ, simply turn the page and allow the journey to begin!

our MESSIAH

Within the gospels, we see four different writers, Matthew, Mark, Luke, and John. Out of these four writers Matthew, Mark, and Luke are named the synoptic gospels because they include many of the same stories, often in a similar sequence and sometimes in identical wording. They stand entirely in contrast to John, whose content is largely distinct. The term synoptic originates from the Greek word *synoptikos*, which means to take a general or comprehensive view. John stands alone as a gospel because although he tells the story of Jesus Christ, his observation of the Messiah is divinely different.

As we observe Matthew's writings, we see that the expression of the term "kingdom of heaven" is mentioned around 32 times. Matthew's reports prove that Jesus Christ is the promised Messiah as he views Christ in his kingship manner. His focus is to portray to the new body of believers and remind current believers that Jesus Christ is the King of Glory and the King of all of the Earth. So in a collective view, the book of Matthew is written to show us not only that Jesus is King of kings, but in order for us to partake in the Kingdom of God, we must receive a particular mindset that enables us to portray the behaviors of a King's child.

Mark views Christ in his posture of servanthood. According to how Mark writes his book, we see Jesus the Messiah coming as a servant. Jesus reveals who he is through what he does, hence we see more miracles in the book of Mark than in any other gospel. The central theme of the gospel of Mark is that Jesus came to Earth to serve. He gave his life in service to mankind, and he lived out his message through aid, therefore, we can follow his actions and learn by his example. We can ultimately learn that through Mark's gospel, we can adapt a servant's mindset that will help us follow in the direction of Christ as we operate in humility. Proverbs 3:34 (NIV) declares, *"He mocks proud mockers but shows favor to the humble and oppressed."*

Luke identifies Christ in his humanity. In the book of Luke, we will find that Jesus Christ's humanity shines through his compassion for all people, more clearly than in any of the other gospels. Luke uses titles such as Son of Man to show the importance of Jesus's humanity. Although we understand Jesus to be fully God, we must also wholly comprehend that he is also fully man, and Luke does a splendid job of portraying this critical fact. Luke shows the humanity of Jesus Christ and his perfection as a human being. He describes in great detail how Jesus Christ was the flawless man who gave the immaculate sacrifice for sin, which was himself, therefore making him the perfect Savior for humanity. As we study

Luke, we can learn that although Jesus Christ was perfect in all of his ways, he also felt the emotions that we feel. The mindset that we eventually gather, as we study Luke, is that of hope. How does this tie into the mind of Christ? Our hope is entangled within the humanity of Christ, for as he walked the Earth and did not sin, he left us a demonstration that our life is ultimately fulfilled in him as we fully submit to him. Hebrews 4:15 (NIV) teaches us, *"For we do not have a high priest who is unable to empathize with our weaknesses, but we have one who has been tempted in every way, just as we are yet he did not sin."*

John shows reverence to the nature of the Messiah. He writes his book so that readers might believe in the name of Jesus Christ. John approaches his writings differently, as he distinctively paints vivid imagery of the divine nature of Jesus Christ. A significant difference in the book of John is that he excludes the origin story of the Messiah's birth but replaces it with describing Jesus' deity. John's desire is for us to see that Jesus is King, Servant, and Son of Man, but also, he is Jesus the Christ. This is vital in understanding God's mind because his deity teaches us his holiness. It is through understanding holiness that we can conform to being holy. As we grasp that holiness means that we are consecrated **(dedicated)**, purified **(refined/washed in the blood of Jesus)**, and sanctified **(set apart)**, we can then walk in the complete mind of God because of our confidence in the divine nature of Jesus Christ.

NOTES

it is
HIS WILL

If each of us had 10,000 tongues, it would not be enough to describe the deity of God. There is no word that has been created to express the depth, width, or divine nature of the God we serve. As we analyze the awesomeness of our Lord, we are able to see that the elements of the Earth are subject to the power of Jesus Christ. This is proven in Mark 4:35-39. In the text, the disciples and Jesus found themselves amid a raging storm while on the boat. The disciples hurried to get the attention of Jesus, and upon grabbing his attention, the Lord uttered the famous words, *"peace be still."* The wind and sea became completely calm as a result of the three words that Jesus Christ articulated.

Colossians 1:16 teaches us that all things were created by him, in him, and for him. The Bible clearly teaches us that God created the universe out of nothing. But why? And how does this relate to us having the mind of God? Well, John teaches us in Revelation 4:11 (NIV), *"You are worthy, our Lord and God, to receive glory and honor and power, for you created all things, and by your will, they were created and have their being."* According to the last phrase, we can conclude that things were created and even exist because it is the will of God.

We must thoroughly analyze what the exact will of God is. There are two clear and very distinct meanings for the term "will of God." Knowing the difference between these two meanings of "the will of God" is crucial to understanding one of the biggest and most perplexing things in the Bible, that is to say, that God is sovereign over all things and yet disapproves of many things. This means that God disapproves of some of what he actually ordains.

The first meaning of the will of God is God's sovereign control of all things. This is known as God's "sovereign will" or his "will of decree." God's will of decree cannot be broken. It always comes to pass. God's sovereignty is as massive as his entire creation. The will of decree is an example of things that happen in mankind's life that are completely out of our control.

While living in North Carolina in 2012, I remember planning a trip to California to visit one of my best friends. My best friend and I had worked out much of the details, and we were excited to hang out and explore the city of Santa Monica, California. However, despite all of the effort we both put into making the trip a reality, factors arose that neither of us could prevent that prohibited that trip from taking place. In 2012, California had a massive Rush Fire documented as the third-largest wildfire recorded in California modern times. This is an example of the sovereign will of God. Sometimes, God will disrupt our plans for specific reasons that are known and sometimes unknown. However, we must never forget, *"All things work together for good to them that love God, to them who are the called according to his purpose."* Romans 8:28 (KJV). As we submit to the will of God, we submit to his desire and purpose for our lives, therefore conforming to his mind. God's will of decree speaks of God's providence.

"All the peoples of the earth are regarded as nothing. He does as he pleases with the powers of heaven and the peoples of the earth. No one can hold back his hand or say to him: "What have you done?""

Daniel 4:35 (NIV)

The other meaning for "the will of God" in the Bible is what we call his "will of command." In this particular will, he instructs us what to do. This is the will of God that we can disobey and fail to do. The will of decree, we do whether we believe in it or not. With the will of command, we have an option to comply or reject because of our liberty. However, rejecting to comply with God's will of command means that we are choosing a life of sin over everlasting life. Choosing a life of sin will ultimately lead us to destruction. As we study the Word of God, we observe that God instructs us to be holy and sanctified. Many of us fail to obey and comply with his desire, willingly choosing to stay in a life of sin, therefore rejecting the overall mind of Christ.

Many times, our rejection to conform to the mind of Christ is because we are unaware that we have access to his mind. As long as we think that our natural mind is able to be converted and do the will of God, we will always function in deception. Converting to the mind of Christ is a spiritual activity and takes real spiritual effort. When we function in the mind of Christ, we fail and reject to do our own will but humbly submit to his.

As we submit to the will of God, it allows us to embrace the communicable wisdom of God, which enables us to live a life that is led under his direction. The wisdom of God comes, primarily from reading and obeying his Word, therefore initiates the process of adapting the Lord's mind. God is infinitely wise, and we are not. Therefore, we must have faith to trust in his divine wisdom for direction even when we do not understand what he is doing. The Lord's wisdom is shown in our individual lives if we were to yield to Christ's mind.

"And we know that all things work together for good to them that love God, to them who are the called according to his purpose."

Romans 8:28 (KJV)

In this scripture, Paul affirms that God works wisely in all things that come into our lives, and through all things, he advances us toward the goal of conforming into the image of Christ.

"For those God foreknew he also predestined to be conformed to the image of his Son, that he might be the firstborn among many brothers and sisters."

Romans 8:29 (NIV)

It should be our assurance day by day to know that God causes all things to move us toward the ultimate goal he has for our lives, which is that we may look like him by accepting his mind.

total DEPENDENCY

One of the first ways to identify God is by acknowledging that he is the one who created all things. Hebrews 11:3 (NIV) says, *"By faith, we understand that the universe was formed at God's command, so that what is seen was not made out of what was visible."* Nothing that God has created can function in its proper state without dependency on God. Since we understand that he created all things, we can also comprehend that nothing can function adequately without God. In Genesis 1:31, God declares that all that he made was good. So we must conclude that man, as well as everything else in the creation, was perfect. The excellent thinking ability which God has given man was perfect. We can see the confidence that God has for man's reasoning and critical thinking before the fall as he trusted Adam to name the woman and all animals to include sea creatures, birds, and insects. Adam was able to exercise his mind in this magnitude because his mind was without blemish. Once sin enters the world through Adam, a breach is established between mankind and God. This breach causes a deterioration in the thought process of the mind, which causes humanity to lose its appropriate functioning of the mind. As man loses his proper ability to think, it then causes the actions that man commits to offend our God, therefore, forcing mankind into a place of sin. However, although sin has entered the world of mankind, our Lord has a plan to unite us with him forever. In the Bible, we see the crucifixion emerge onto the scene. The crucifixion and resurrection are known to be the most significant miracles that Jesus performed.

Jesus illustrates miracles of healing in all four gospels. Our Lord is a remarkable God, and we witness, through the text, that he distinguishes himself through his deity and actions. We see proof of his deity and distinguishing acts as Christ walks on water and fills the belly of five thousand men, not to include women and children, with two fish and five loaves of bread.

I love that within all of the splendor, majesty, and magnificence of Jesus Christ the Messiah, he has made himself available to us. As we closely follow the miracles of Jesus within the gospels, we can easily agree with Dr. Wayne Grudem that miracles are defined as a less common kind of God's activity in which he arouses peoples' awe and wonder and bears witness to himself. This definition takes into consideration God's providence and ability to preserve, control, and govern all things. God's creation of all things, including the complexity of man's mind, shows his wisdom and power. The beauty about our creator is that he has permitted us to have access to all things that pertain to life and godliness, which includes his presence, his authority, and even his mind. Jesus Christ desires for us to be and think just as he does. To live and think in victory means to lean on and completely trust in Christ.

NOTES

what is
the MIND
of CHRIST?

To understand the mind of Christ, we must take a look into who Jesus was before he was born into human flesh. As the eternal Son of God, Jesus enjoyed the glory and praise of all the angels of Heaven. Christ chose to temporarily part-with the magnificence, splendor, and brilliance of Heaven so that we could dwell with him in eternity. The sacrifice of Christ would lose all its force as an expression of God's love if Jesus did not exist before his incarnation. Christ preexisted all of creation and was foreknown by God, not only before his incarnation but also before the world's foundation.

Can you imagine the beauty of Heaven? Can you visualize the walls of Heaven, adorned with stones of every kind; streets made of gold, Jesus' throne, the sea that resembles glass, and the angels with six wings that fly around God day and night declaring his holiness? Without question, Heaven must be a beautiful sight to see and dwell in. Nevertheless, Jesus Christ gave it all up, made himself of no reputation, and took upon him the form of a servant, which made him to be in the likeness of men. Therefore, being found in the likeness of man, he humbled himself and became obedient unto death, even the humiliating death of the cross. Jesus' love for fallen mankind caused Him to willingly lay aside His glory and His form as God and take upon Himself the form of a servant. This does not mean that Jesus laid aside His deity. Instead, He chose to set aside all of his self-rights: His right to be recognized as the Creator of the world, His right to be treated with honor and respect, and His right to be loved. We can observe that this level of self-denial is a humbling procedure. If we, as servants of King Jesus, want to be united with him forever and be like Jesus Christ, our process begins with our thinking.

Thinking is comprised of how one perceives actions and events and how one responds to the activities and events of life. Christ desires that we perceive things the same way that he perceived them and respond to actions and events the way he responded to them. Jesus desires that we operate with the same grace in dealing with one another and our enemies that he operated in. For we are instructed in Psalm 37:37a (KJV) to *"Mark the perfect man, and behold the upright."* Jesus Christ is the perfect man, and he desires for us to walk in a life of perfection, just as he has. The misconception is that we have to live a life of defeat, a life catered to sin, and a life full of mistakes and mess-ups. These are lies birthed from Satan. Although we have been born into sin and shaped in iniquity (Psalm 51:5), when we surrender and submit to the Word of God as we give our lives to him, we take on a new identity.

"Therefore, if anyone is in Christ, he is a new creation; old things have passed away; behold, all things have become new."

2 Corinthians 5:17 (NKV)

We do not have to stay in the marred image of Adam. As new creatures in Christ, everything about us becomes transformed, including our thinking. When we receive Christ, our thinking embraces the mind of Christ and begins to take on this new image.

God has so many wonderful things planned for us. Jeremiah 29:11 (NKJV) declares, *"I know the thoughts that I think toward you, says the Lord, thoughts of peace and not of evil to bring you into an expected end."* To exercise God's many amazing plans for our lives, we must submit to his revealed will. We will not know everything that God has for us nor the totality of God's mind because God is an infinite being, and we are finite or limited beings within nature. Therefore, we depend on God's active communication with us in Scripture and His illumination of scripture for our true knowledge and understanding. Within this sense, we can comprehend Isaiah 55:8-9.

"For my thoughts are not your thoughts, neither are your ways my ways, says the Lord. For as the heavens are higher than the earth, so are my ways higher than your ways, and my thoughts than your thoughts."

Isaiah 55:8-9 (KJV)

As we analyze this text, we understand that thoughts are to mean the plan of God, and ways are to mean the path or direction of God. This scripture teaches us that the plans God has for us is higher and greater than any plan we can

31

create for ourselves, and the paths God takes us on is not the path we would have selected for ourselves.

Typically, if we are honest with ourselves, our desired paths would have little to no hardship. The intensity that one endures as a child of God is very high, and the persecution that one suffers is strenuous. To effectively deal with and endure hardship as a good soldier, which we were commanded to do in 2 Timothy 2:3, our mindset must be conditioned to handle this type of warfare. Our ability to handle warfare comes through our practice of guarding our hearts and minds.

"And the peace of God, which surpasses all understanding, will guard your hearts and minds through Christ Jesus."
Philippians 4:7 (NKJV)

The peace of God keeps us beyond our power and ability to understand and explain. According to C.H. Spurgeon, the peace of God is defined as the eternal composure of the well-contented God. The peace of God is never separated from the atonement of God. The atonement of God allows us to be at peace with him. I cannot show the peace of God. However, I would direct you to the cross of Calvary, where the peace of God has been made available for you and me.

Although we may not understand God or the mind of God exhaustively, we can know God's true attributes and character. To say this does not imply that we know everything about God or his qualities, but it is in our knowledge of God, through the Scriptures, that we can know the thoughts of God that he has revealed to man. To know the truth of God does not speak of simply knowing facts or actions about God, but it is to know God himself. Within the ordinary English language, we draw a division between knowing facts and knowing persons. To know God in person is to have had an encounter and experience with him. Thus, to know God is to know Him intimately, meaning to be "One" with him.

"On that day you will realize that I am in my Father, and you are in me, and I am in you."

John 14:20 (NIV)

To put it plainly, through the Holy Spirit, we would know a life that is deep in relationship, a shared life, and union with God.

NOTES

so a
MAN THINKETH

The central theme of every man's actions is surrounded by his thoughts. Our thoughts are vital to our way of living and the way that we perceive ourselves. To ensure that we identify ourselves in the way God sees us, we must endeavor to have a spiritual mind. As we surrender to the mind of Christ and his will, we begin the process of transformation from our carnal mind into the mind of Jesus Christ. As transformation occurs, we will start to think, feel, judge, respond, and react more and more like Christ. Romans 12:2 (KJV) says, *"And be not conformed to this world: but be ye transformed by the renewing of your mind, that ye may prove what is that good, and acceptable and perfect, will of God."* We can conclude that where the mind goes, our actions follow.

One of the main ways the Holy Spirit instructs and transforms us is through His written Word. As we study, reflect, and meditate on the written Word of God, the transformation process begins to change our minds and spirit.

The mind is the seat of all intellect and the control center for our thoughts and actions. It is essential for us to realize that we do not have to succumb to every thought we think. We have the power to redirect our thoughts. Paul teaches us in Philippians 4:8 (KJV) that we should *"think on things that are true, honest, just, pure, lovely, good report, virtue and anything that is praiseworthy."* These traits are seeds that the Holy Spirit will cultivate, and he will cause them to spring forth in our everyday living. Much of what the believer battles originates in the mind, therefore causing the mind to be the battlefield. Many of us have lost consecutive battles before we step into warfare because we have not trained our minds to perceive conflict how the Lord perceives conflict. If we are not careful about what we think, we will lose every battle we face.

Negative thoughts, promiscuous thoughts, ideas of quitting, crime, lying, envy, thoughts of not being good enough, thoughts of poverty, ungodly philosophies, false religion, arrogance, pride, and any thought that is not in agreement with Philippians 4:8 is an enemy to the believer and should be brought into captivity. Plainly put, there are thoughts that we should not agree with or allow to take hold of our minds as children of God. I have found that frequently, because of life's circumstances, one of the thoughts that so often grabs our mind is worrying. When worrying attempts to penetrate our thought process, we must submit our minds over to our Lord's providential care.

"Therefore I tell you, do not worry about your life, what you will eat or drink; or about your body, what you will wear. Is not life more than food, and the body more than clothes? Look at the birds of the air; they

do not sow or reap or store away in barns, and yet your heavenly Father
feeds them. Are you not much more valuable than they? Can any one of
you by worrying add a single hour to your life? And why do you worry
about clothes? See how the flowers of the field grow. They do not labor or
spin. Yet I tell you that not even Solomon in all his splendor was dressed
like one of these. If that is how God clothes the grass of the field, which
is here today and tomorrow is thrown into the fire, will he not much more
clothe you—you of little faith? So do not worry, saying, what shall we
eat? Or what shall we drink? Or what shall we wear? For the pagans
run after all these things, and your heavenly Father knows that you need
them. "

Matthew 6:25-32 (NIV)

Satan has three common moves that he uses against the
believer. These three moves open doors to many other traps.
The adversary, our enemy, Satan, never neglects to appeal to
the lust of the flesh, the lust of the eyes, and the pride of life (1 John
2:16). Every attack on the flesh begins with your mind. As it
attacks your mind, it gives birth to desires and lust that leads
toward actions. This is why it is imperative to take note of
the thoughts you are having and immediately cast down the
thoughts that are not of God. We must weigh each thought
against the word of God, and if a thought fails to pass the
inspection, it does not equate with the plan of God.

Bringing every thought into captivity that does not align
itself with the obedience of Christ is spiritual warfare. Paul
teaches us that though we walk in the flesh, we do not war
after the flesh. This implies that we cannot rely on carnal
thinking or manmade plans to bring victory into our lives.
We must understand that our carnal thinking is powerless
against the attacks of the devil. When we notice thoughts

in our minds that do not align with God's word, we must immediately go into prayer, study, and mediation of God's word and replace our wrong thoughts with the thoughts that Christ has commanded us to think.

NOTES

CONFORMING to the LORD'S WAY

A mind of Christ is a mind that is yielded to the Spirit of God. It displays the fruit of the Spirit, which enables the mind to be fully submitted in love without limitations. As a child, I loved to spend time hanging around the elderly, gleaning from their life's experiences. During my time with them, I heard certain things I now realize was not always fitting to the mind of Christ. One day, my grandmother, her friend, and I went to church for revival. As we were parking at the church, someone sped ahead of us and took the parking spot where my grandmother was about to park. My grandmother then blurted out, "I can't stand people. I really don't like people at all." As a young boy, I laughed really hard at how agitated she was. As I became older, I now realize that this is not the mind of Christ.

Despite the situation or our frustrations, we must learn and have the ability to love beyond our emotional distresses. The life of Christ teaches us to love without limitations. Our close observation of his life will reveal the level of humility he endured to portray the love he had for us. In Christian theology, we learn of a term called Hypostatic Union, which describes the unity of Christ's humanity and divinity in one hypostasis. Plainly put, Jesus Christ was 100% God and 100% man at the same time. Within all of his divinity, he decided to also make himself human without forfeiting his divinity. So God, the creator of all things, humbled himself to take on a bodily image like ours so that he could die for us. As a result of his death and resurrection, we can be united with him forever and always. This is an expression of love without limitations.

As we show our love for God that carries no barriers, we learn to humbly and willingly comply to his authority because we love him. Our love for God is shown through our obedience to him.

"If you love me, keep my commandments."
John 14:15 (NKJV)

As we exercise our love for God by obeying and keeping his commandments, we are displaying our submission to God. An individual cannot say that they love God or that God lives within them if they fail to submit to God's word. The word of the Lord does not conform to any individual, but we as believers must adapt and allow the word of God to transform us. The transformation process does not mean that our physical bodies will begin to change. It means that our spiritual bodies will be born again, and we will begin a new way of living and thinking. Our new way of living is saturated in the mind of Christ, and makes our behavior contrary to how we once behaved. We will see ourselves loving effortlessly, willingly submitting to God's word, and sacrificing our pride for the exaltation of God. These traits help us maintain a mind that produces a yielded spirit.

NOTES

SURRENDER

When we truly yield our spirit to the Spirit of God, we ultimately surrender to God. To surrender to God means relinquishing ownership and control over what we feel is ours: our time, property, rights, money, family, and even our thoughts. As we surrender to God, we acknowledge that we actually belong to Him. Submitting to God allows us to let go of whatever has kept us from wanting God's ways above all things. To truly surrender to God, the first thing we must completely let go of is thinking.

Our thinking controls our actions, our actions manipulate our bodies, but our bodies are vessels of God. Our bodies do not belong to us. Our minds do not belong to us; everything we are made of belongs to God. We must relinquish complete control of everything, forsaking all to follow Jesus Christ. We must be willing to allow God to take over. Often, because we have been hurt by people and let down by certain events in our lives, we have a propensity to put walls around our hearts as a defense mechanism. We also purposely harden our hearts to justify the hurt we feel. This is not evidence of a mind that has been transformed to the mind of God but rather a mind that has conformed to the ways of the world.

Failure to submit ourselves to the mind of Christ can negatively impact our everyday life, even our health. A believer's health is not defined by how happy, prosperous, or physically healthy we are. Christian health is ultimately determined by how sincerely we wave our flag of surrender to the mind of Christ. If we want a change in our life, it comes when we totally surrender our mind to his. Surrendering our mind to God is deeper than what we think, but how we think. Some think that when you come to Christ, you have to leave your mind behind, but our faith is not irrational.

According to a collegiate university's research, an average child will watch 8,000 murders on TV before finishing elementary school. By the age of eighteen, the average American has seen 200,000 acts of violence on TV, including 40,000 murders. In reality, our minds get saturated with violence, swearing, and sex constantly. Since our minds operate like computers, they retain what they receive. Ultimately, we learn that we reinforce what has been repeated in our minds.

This is why we must exercise submitting ourselves to the Lord in every moment of every day. Surrendering our minds and thoughts to God must become our lifestyle. Whenever negative thoughts desire to penetrate our space, we must cut them off and immediately give them to God.

"This I recall to my mind, therefore have I hope. It is of the Lord's

mercies that we are not consumed, because his compassions fail not. They are new every morning great is thy faithfulness."

Lamentations 3:21-23 (KJV)

Do not carry negative thoughts around with you. Thoughts that do not align with God's thoughts take up space for God's grace and favor.

Having the mind of Christ is essential to living in the Spirit and resisting the world's temptations. Therefore, our ability to successfully overcome temptations are anchored in living holy. The temptations that we often face are based on our human needs. Satan wants us to satisfy those needs with sinful choices, but God wants us to give Him our needs and trust Him to meet them in His time and in His way. Therefore, we should ask God to turn each temptation into a signal to seek Him and learn His ways. You can always tell where God wants to bless you the most by what your greatest struggle is. It is wisdom to replace the things that draw you into wrongful thoughts and actions with activities that strengthen your spirit.

"I say then: Walk in the Spirit, and you shall not fulfill the lust of the flesh. For the flesh lust against the Spirit, and the Spirit against the flesh; and these are contrary to one another, so that you do not do the things that you wish."

Galatians 5:16-17 (NKJV)

Living holy is based around the mind of Christ. Holiness enables us to access the character in which Christ operated. The ability to think like Christ is imperative for righteous living.

NOTES

_____

_____

_____

_____

_____

_____

_____

_____

_____

_____

_____

_____

_____

_____

_____

_____

_____

_____

_____

_____

_____

_____

what is in
YOUR HEART?

O ne of the greatest gifts that God has given mankind is the human mind. Within our minds, we can think, reason, learn, recall, and choose. Your thoughts become the essence of who you are. This idea is expressed in Proverbs 23:7a (NKJV) as it declares, *"For as he thinks in his heart, so is he."* The heart's thoughts shape the reality of who a person really is, which will ultimately impact their actions. If we acknowledge God's method, we will see that God was always ultimately in pursuit of the heart. God desires that our hearts are pure, tender, and actively and earnestly seeking after him.

> *"Create in me a clean heart, O God, and renew a right spirit within me."*
>
> Psalm 51:10 (NKJV)

David utters this desire because he acknowledges that there are some impurities in his life, and because of that, he needs God to create in him a clean heart. David understands that God can only clean the heart. If the heart is cleansed, we can be sure that the thoughts that lead to our actions will be clean. Let us be sure to grow from David's statement and utilize his words with truth as we so carefully go before God. Let us ask God to clean our hearts, for if our hearts are clean, our actions will be pleasing before God.

"And I will give you a new heart, and a new spirit I will put within you. And I will remove the heart of stone from your flesh and give you a heart a heart of flesh."
Ezekiel 36:26 (NKJV)

Here we see that God is getting ready to perform a spiritual transformation. This transformation comes by way of the new covenant, which is fulfilled in Jesus Christ. The Lord desires to give his people a new heart that will transform them from the inside out. This spiritual transformation will help his people think differently, which will lead to a new way of living.

"Blessed are the pure in heart, for they shall see God."
Matthew 5:8 (NKJV)

If our heart is clean, unstained, blameless, and innocent of defilements and wickedness, we will receive the most fulfilling reward we could ever imagine. God's desire for our lives is that our hearts will be purified of all unrighteousness so that no barrier hinders us from complete and total intimacy with the Lord. Within our intimate moments with God, he releases the unattainable secrets and keys to total victory over the enemy. In our intimacy with the Lord, we experience the fullness of his joy and receive the strength we need to overcome the wiles of the devil.

"With my whole heart have I sought You; Oh, let me not wander from your commandments!"

Psalm 119:10 (NKJV)

In this scripture, the Psalmist positions himself to seek the Lord's care with his whole heart extensively. If we are going to behave in pure holiness, we must first desire to respond, act, speak, or conduct ourselves in the way the Lord requires in the situations we find ourselves. Responding to any situation without seeking God is a sinful act.

"Trust in the Lord with all your heart, and lean not to your own understanding; in all your ways acknowledge Him, and He shall direct your paths."

Proverbs 3:5-6 (NKJV)

As we read the Bible, we learn about many individuals who experienced success in their endeavors because they surrendered to the mind of Christ. Let us examine four gentlemen, in particular, starting with the father of faith, Abraham.

ABRAHAM

Despite the pagan worship of Abraham's ancestors, Abraham was called into covenant with God in the early part of Genesis 12. He distinguished himself as far different from his ancestors as he obeyed God to leave the land that his faithless extended family occupied in Mesopotamia. He obeyed God again when he left the land of Harran (Acts 7:1-4). Abraham put his trust in God's guidance rather than emotional feelings or others' opinions. Abraham was willing to go wherever God led him, and this shows his total dependency on God.

Abraham's dependency on God is displayed to us as he obeyed and trusted God throughout his life. Through Abraham's early life, God instructed him where to settle and caused him to experience victory in an area that seemed impossible. At the age of 75, God promised Abraham a son. Initially, I would imagine that he was excited and told many people about the promise God made him. After 24 years of waiting with expectation but still no sign of the promise, Abraham had to be reminded of the promise so that he didn't abort the covenant God made with him. Sometimes, we have to be reminded of the promise God made with us, so we don't allow doubt to abort the covenant God made with us. The recap reminds us to trust that what God says, he will perform. Even though we may not see our promise, yet we must trust God.

"Abraham believed God and it was credited to him as righteousness."
Romans 4:3 (NKJV)

MOSES

Moses was a man of many insecurities and self-doubts, but God still used him to lead the Israelites to liberty. As the Israelites left Egypt, they faced insurmountable obstacles, and the entire camp looked to Moses for help and direction. Instead of Moses depending upon himself, he looks to God for guidance, and God instructs Moses to use his staff. As a result of Moses depending on God, we see supernatural manifestations such as the parting of the Red Sea. When faced with this challenge, all of Israel began to doubt Moses, but Moses trusted God.

We must learn how to trust God despite what others around us and those in our inner circle believe. It is because Moses trusted in God that God parted the Red Sea, and the Israelites were able to cross over into the Promised Land on dry ground. The enemies that followed them were drowned in the same sea that the Israelites thought they would never cross. This event was pivotal for the children of Israel because it set them free from 430 years of slavery. Sometimes, what we feel may be a barrier is only a means to elevate our faith in God and the same tool that God will use to destroy our enemy.

JOSEPH

Joseph epitomizes dependency on God in difficulty. If we are to unite with Christ Jesus truly, we must prove our commitment to him by remaining steadfast in trying situations. When we stand with God throughout the storms in our lives, we make a bold statement that we believe and trust in God. We forsake sensational feelings and depend on God to lead us into the path of righteousness. Joseph is a prime example of that, as from a young man, he believed that God had a plan for his life. In Joseph's dreams, God ensured that he would elevate him to a position of power and authority. Although this seemed to be great news for Joseph because it signified divine blessing, it stirred up hatred and malice in Joseph's brothers' hearts. As a result of their jealousy, Joseph's brothers initially began to plot Joseph's murder but settled for selling him into slavery.

Joseph was sold to Potiphar and was placed in a position of high esteem. After a while, Potiphar's wife began to take an interest in Joseph. His refusal of Potiphar's wife's advances was admirable, as he reminded her of the trust that Potiphar had in him and described that the relationship that she sought after with him was immoral, wicked, and sinful. After verbally resisting her repeatedly and avoiding her, he then decides to flee from her after she physically assaulted him. This action caused Potiphar's wife to lie on Joseph, and her lies land him in prison. While in prison, Joseph met two of Pharaoh's officials who were also incarcerated, the chief cupbearer and the chief baker. While Joseph was in prison, he interprets dreams for many different individuals, including the chief cupbearer. After a while, the chief cupbearer was released from prison. When Pharaoh began to have dreams, the chief cupbearer remembered Joseph. Joseph was freed from prison to work in the house of Pharaoh and then elevated to being the second in command.

As you can see from this brief synopsis of Joseph's life, he had many ups and downs. However, Joseph never reneged on what God gave him in a dream. Sometimes, faithfulness to God and his words seem to set us on a course where circumstances get worse rather than better. In those moments, we must remember that God will be faithful to his promises. Truly understanding the mind of God, in the essence that he loves us and truly wants the best for us, will allow us to trust in his divine plan for our lives.

PAUL

Paul was admirable when it came to trusting God during

turmoil. In the society we live in, it is common to see many people panic while in hardship. However, the God of all grace has instructed us to *be strong and be of good courage, fear not, nor be afraid."* Deuteronomy 31:6a (KJV) At one point in his life, Paul was a prisoner on a ship doomed to wreck. Although the ship was destined to be wrecked, Paul knew his position in Christ.

As believers, it is imperative that we understand what God thinks of us. Grasping the concept of how the Messiah views us is a vital asset to understanding the love and destiny God has for us. Although we may not fully comprehend his plan, we can fully trust and have faith in his leadership, plans, and desires.

While everyone around Paul was deeply terrified, Paul trusted God and his Word. As a result, everyone survived the shipwreck just as the angel declared.

I assure you, this day, that whatever word God has spoken over your life will come to pass, regardless of the turmoil you face. Trust God and his word. When we fully submit and trust him at his word, we think as he thinks, which is to perceive and believe things to be as God said they would be.

NOTES

HIS MIND

One of the most astounding illuminating facts in the New Testament is that we can achieve the mind of Christ. Paul testifies about this truth in Philippians 2:5 (KJV) *"Let this mind be in you, which was also in Christ Jesus."* As we dissect this verse to grab a full understanding of what Paul is describing, we must first see that Paul uses the word "Let." This alludes to the fact that we must permit the mind of Christ into our minds. How do we adapt the mind of Christ? We must be willing to accept his concepts. Christ often introduced bold, new ideas and perceptions. One of his most famous teachings was on the topic of love. His teachings admonished us to love despite periods of hate, chaos, and conflict. His teachings taught us that we must have a new heart filled with His intents and desires. Our subconscious minds must adapt to the leading of the mind of Christ.

There is a distinctive difference between the conscious mind and the subconscious mind. Many psychologists say that the conscious mind comprises willpower, logical thinking, and critical thinking. In contrast, the subconscious mind consists of our beliefs, emotions, habits, values, perspectives, long-term memories, and imaginations. Our subconscious mind controls our reactions, our responses, and even our dreams. God intends that our minds reflect his mind, our actions reflect his actions, and our reactions reflect his reactions.

In Matthew 5, we find what is commonly referred to as the "Be-Attitudes." Through these verses, Christ instructs us how to conduct ourselves as believers.

"Blessed are the poor in spirit, for theirs is the kingdom of heaven.
Blessed are those who mourn, for they will be comforted.
Blessed are the meek, for they will inherit the earth.
Blessed are those who hunger and thirst for righteousness, for they will be filled.
Blessed are the merciful, for they will be shown mercy.
Blessed are the pure in heart, for they will see God.
Blessed are the peacemakers, for they will be called children of God.
Blessed are those who are persecuted because of righteousness, for theirs is the kingdom of heaven.
Blessed are you when people insult you, persecute you and falsely say all kinds of evil against you because of me.
Rejoice and be glad, because great is your reward in heaven, for in the same way they persecuted the prophets who were before you."
Matthew 5:3-12 (NIV)

The beatitudes consist of the responses and behaviors Christ commands us to have as residents of the kingdom of heaven.

Our subconscious mind must submit to the level of sanctification until we can joyfully bless those who persecute us and pray for those who speak evil against us. We must display traits of peace, mercy, gentleness, and complete dependence on God. A lack of these traits reveals a lack of submission to the mind of Christ.

The Bible goes into extreme detail as it describes what the word "mind" means. As writer Nancy Missler points out in her article, What is in our mind?, as we initiate the process of allowing God to transform our minds, we find that if we were to submit to the Lord, He would guide our minds by his Word. It is similar to how a rider guides his horse. The rider understands that the specific destination he has in mind for the horse. If the horse follows the rider's guidance, the horse has submitted to the guidance of the rider. If the horse rebels, the horse is stubborn and is kicking against the pricks. The rider's responsibility is to direct, instruct, and control where the horse goes. The rider is also responsible for the horse's wellbeing, making the rider the Master of the horse. It is not the horse's responsibility to lead the rider, but the horse's responsibility is to follow the guidance of its Master. If the horse refuses to follow the instruction of its Master, then it is accurate to say that the horse is in a rebellious mindset and, therefore, his actions are a reflection of his state of mind.

We must carefully inspect what we allow into our spirits. Whatever we allow into our spirits influence our mind and attitude, which affects our actions. Our minds and attitude are always affected by three things: what we see, hear, and say. These three portals are vital to the mindset of any individual.

"The lamp of the body is the eye. If your eye is good, your whole body will be full of light. But if your eye is bad, your whole body will be full of darkness."

Matthew 6:22-23 (NKJV)

To have a good eye means to continually view what is holy; a bad eye views what is unholy. The eyes are the doorway to our minds, and whatever our minds constantly think upon, our actions will soon follow. If we are going to be pure and holy, we must be intentional about guarding our eyes. This includes carefully selecting the movies we watch, books we read, and internet sites we visit.

Two other facets that affect our mind is what we hear and what we say. Proverbs 18:21 (NKJV) declares, *"The power of life and death is in the tongue."* Words that are spoken over someone's life has great capability to guide them, either leading them into a wise or evil direction. Words can build a person or destroy them. If a person sits under godly parents who are faithful to the Lord's teaching, they will more than likely pursue to live in a positive, godly manner. Likewise, if someone is consuming ungodly teaching and conversations, their lives will be impacted in an ungodly way. This is because of the influence that positive and negative conversations have on the mind.

As we remain cautious to guard our eyes, ears, and language, we must guard our minds. As we fight against the enemy to present ourselves holy and acceptable unto God, we must indulge firmly in the word of God. A person who does not know God's word will have much difficulty protecting himself against the enemy. Their minds will continually be bombarded with ungodly thoughts with no restraint.

As a kid, football was huge in my family. My dad was a legendary coach, and my cousin and my godbrother were both epic high school players in my hometown. Needless to say, I was always around football, gleaning the knowledge of the game. Every Saturday morning, my cousin and godbrother would come over to my house and watch the film of their Friday night game to critique their efforts with hopes of becoming better players. As they studied their efforts, I watched every move, play, and mistake. I saw football every Friday night, Saturday morning, and Sunday evening as my father watched the NFL football games after church. I also saw football throughout the week as I attended my cousin and godbrother's football practice.

Along with watching football so much, I also heard about football a lot. I often listened as my father coached my cousin and godbrother on what they could do better and what they did well. I would also hear about my family's mindset and the mental toughness that it took to play this game.

As a result of constantly watching and hearing about football, I spoke about football regularly. I dreamed of becoming great and often shared my thoughts about the game I fell in love with. I thought about football all the time. Even as an adult, I still enjoy watching and playing football. My environment cultivated my mindset about football.

Understanding the gateways that are open in our lives has a significant effect on our lives' direction. We are told in 1 Peter 1:13 (NKJV), *Therefore gird up the loins of your mind, be sober, and rest your hope fully upon the grace that is to be brought to you at the revelation of Jesus Christ;* As obedient children, we do not conduct ourselves after our flesh. We are to be holy, as he who has called us to be holy is holy.

If we continuously observe and hear about a variable, it will become apart of who we are. As believers, we must pay close attention to every variable we allow to influence us.

NOTES

DISCIPLINE

We must put forth every effort to memorize God's word. In Psalm 119:11 (KJV), David says, *"Thy word have I hid in my heart, that I may not sin against thee."* We can conclude from the text that David has memorized God's word to give him the strength to flee temptation. In the book "Chosen," Archbishop Lorenzo Peterson suggests that we toil to learn God's word. As we learn his word and put it to memory, we can have the word of God readily available as a weapon effective in spiritual warfare.

When I first gave my life to Christ, I had a meaningful conversation with my cousin, who was already mature in the Lord. She brought a vital perspective into reality for me. She pointed out that every soldier should always know their weapons. When a soldier enlists in the Army, they go through a series of trainings that help develop them into good soldiers. There are two aspects of trainings that drill sergeants focus on. The first dimension is discipline. It does not matter how well a soldier can perform a specific task if he lacks discipline. Discipline is a result of the constraints to which an individual allows their minds to submit. As the mind surrenders to the discipline enforced, the individual's character transforms, which then converts our actions. A changed mindset will always lead to changed behavior.

The second aspect is weapon knowledge. While in basic training, soldiers take time to learn everything there is to know about their weapons. Soldiers must disassemble and reassemble their weapons hundreds of times. As they do so, they study the capabilities of the weapon. They educate themselves on how to hold their weapons, how much the weapons weigh, and the damage their weapons are capable of causing. A soldier must know everything there is to know about their weapon.

As believers, we must also know everything there is to know about our weapons. Our weapon is the Word of God. In Matthew 4, as Jesus was tempted, the weapon he used to fight against Satan was the word of God. We must hold God's word in our hearts and minds. God's word should be held with much esteem and admiration, as it is infallible. His word never fails, and it is the only thing that is guaranteed.

> *"Forever, O Lord, your word is settled in heaven."*
> Psalm 119:89 (NKJV)

> *"Heaven and earth will pass away, but My words will by no means pass away.*
> Matthew 24:35 (NKJV)

The word of God has the power to deliver and set free. 2 Corinthians 3:17 NKJV testifies, *"Where the Spirit of the Lord is there is liberty."* Our minds do not have to be trapped by toxic thoughts or ideas.

Paul teaches us that when toxic thoughts come into our minds, we can cast them down. 2 Corinthians 10:5 (KJV) says, *"Casting down imaginations, and every high thing that exalteth itself against the knowledge of God, and bringing into captivity every thought to the obedience of Christ."* This process is much like how our kidneys function. The kidneys are designed to filter out poison, waste, debris, and filth.

"The acts of the flesh are obvious: sexual immorality, not being pure, taking part in sexual sins, worshiping gods, doing witchcraft, hating, making trouble, being jealous, having discord, being selfish, making people angry with each other, causing divisions among people, feeling envy, being drunk, having wild and wasteful parties, and doing things like these. I warn you now as I warned you before: Those who do these things will not inherit God's kingdom."

Galatians 5:19-21 (NIV)

We also learn that in Matthew 15:19-20a (NIV), *"For out of the heart come evil thoughts: murder, adultery, sexual immorality, theft, false testimony, slander. These are what defile a person."* For our minds and bodies to be pure, we must constantly purge them of filth. Just as our kidneys do this for our bodies, our minds are empowered with this same grace.

CARNAL MINDS

Many may feel as though they do not need the mind of Christ. Some may think that his thoughts are too high to obtain, leaving them to be complacent with living a life that renders no victory. The fact that we are in a constant struggle for victory confirms that we are in warfare with an opposing force. We must choose our sides. Romans 8:7 (KJV) states, *"Because the carnal mind is enmity against God: for it is not subject to the law of God, neither can be."* A carnal mind is focused upon fleshly desires; it is a dangerous mind to have. This type of mind invites death into our lives and wages war against God. We cannot please God with a carnal mind. A mind that is not submitted to Christ is a mind that refuses to be crucified with Christ. When we fail to submit to the mind of God, we are embracing the carnal mind. As we embrace the carnal mind, we are therefore casting down the kingdom of God. By the nature of God, this is a sin. The carnal mind separates us from God. Most people are concerned about the physical death while completely overlooking the truth that real death is the absence of Christ within our lives. The only way for us to live at peace with God is to submit our minds to the Spirit of God.

"For to be carnally minded is death; but to be spiritually minded is life and peace."

Romans 8:6 (KJV)

We must live by the Spirit of God, although we are finite beings. Our flesh is at war against God because our flesh does not like to be rejected. The idea of pain, affliction, suffering, and crucifixion is a feeling that humans naturally desire to flee from because it never appeases the flesh or desires to surrender totally to the Lord Jesus Christ.

"Those who are Christ's have crucified the flesh with its passions and desires."

Galatians 5:24 (NKJV)

Many struggle with carnal thoughts because sin is pleasurable to the flesh, and they are not willing to relinquish this temporary satisfaction.

However, the more we grow in God, the more distasteful sin becomes. Although we believe in God, we must understand that God has not disconnected us from our flesh. Therefore, the struggle between our spirit and flesh will always wage war on our minds. As our flesh speaks to our minds through its contact with the world, our faith reaches for God in the spirit realm, desiring him to tell our minds what to do through our spirit.

NOTES

HOW will
YOU RESPOND?

In John 14:6, Jesus profoundly states, *"I am the way and the truth and the life. No one comes to the Father except through me."* This statement has caused an uproar for many non-believers because it clarifies that the only way to experience the fullness of God the Father is through accepting and believing in Jesus Christ. The Roman Government Empire also met this concept with much opposition. As a result, they persecuted the first and second-century churches because Christians refused to deny or compromise their belief in Jesus Christ.

One of the most unmoveable disciples of the faith was named Bishop Polycarp. Polycarp was a leader in the church, and one day, hate and hostility broke out against the believers of Jesus Christ. The authorities arrested Polycarp and commanded him to deny his God. Polycarp refused, and the authorities brought him to a massive arena to face the government officials. Once there, the governor of the

Roman province pleaded with the bishop to curse Christ so that he could be released. To this request, Polycarp replied, *"Eighty and six years have I served Him, and he never did any injury; how then can I blaspheme my King and my Savior?"* Polycarp knew the consequences of his response, yet he refused to deny God. As a result, he was burned alive.

There were many martyrs of the Christian faith in the first and second-century churches. Thousands of men and women were burned alive and used as streetlights, beheaded, scourged until their veins and arteries were exposed, tarred, and many other inhumane, fatal punishments. However, the Christian faith has stood the test of time, declaring Jesus Christ as the Messiah despite the cost.

Growing up, I often heard saints declare, *"For God, I'll live, and for God, I'll die."* In today's society, you don't hear this phrase too often. Perhaps, people have forgotten this firm belief. Paul teaches us that our bodies are living sacrifices, meaning that we are to make our total selves an available offering unto God (Romans 12:1). When we live up to this standard, we operate in obedience and full submission to God. As we navigate through life as believers of Jesus Christ, we must not be naïve to think that we will not encounter persecution or testing. It is imperative that we understand the difference between the two so that we are aware of how to win, overcome, and maintain the mind of Christ.

ENDURING TESTS. SURVIVING PERSECUTION.

When we are persecuted, the overall goal of the enemy is to demolish our faith. Testing aims to manifest our weaknesses and exploit them. Whether we are being tested or persecuted, we win by allowing God's word to become our life. The process of His word becoming our life begins with the transformation of our thinking.

The Hall of Famers of the Christian faith are known for what they make it through, not the accolades they receive. Many of the Bible characters we know and look up have an extensive track record of enduring trouble. Through their stories, we come to understand that our difficulties reveal the power of God. God expects us to come out of troubling seasons better than we went in. However, how we leave trouble depends on the mindset we have in the midst of it.

Hanania, Mishael, and Azariah, who bore the Babylonian names Shadrach, Meshach, and Abednego, can tell you about the importance of maintaining a mind that is surrendered to God when faced with trouble. These three young men had the opportunity to endure a fiery furnace for God's name's sake. Although it may seem dreadful and inhumane, God never prohibited them from going into the flames, yet he protected them, proved them, and proved his name while they were in the midst of the fire.

I've endured quite a bit of testing, and I'm sure you have too. I've learned that we never stop being tested; we merely graduate from one level to the next. Due to the pressures of life, I can testify, with confidence, about God's character. In 2013, I was a senior in school at North Carolina Central University. Unfortunately, I did not finish my senior year of college. My family had begun to expand, and my son was born during the same months of my final exams. This new addition to our family caused a great deal of economic stress. Additionally, as a newlywed, I was still learning how to manage my marriage.

After being kicked out of college during senior year, I found a job at a department store. For about a month, things seemed to be improving. Then, in January 2014, I began to see blood in my urine. After being examined, the doctors informed me that I had a kidney infection, contaminated blood, and Methicillin-resistant Staphylococcus aureus (MRSA). MRSA is a bacterium that causes infection in different parts of the body. It is challenging to treat because it resists many common antibiotics. After my results came back, the doctors immediately inserted a PICC line in my arm to give me medication because oral medicine was not strong enough to ease the symptoms I experienced.

After getting out of the hospital, my wife and I separated, my job laid me off, and I had just moved. At the age of 24, I had been kicked out of college, had a son, my health was declining, my wife, kids, and I were separated, and I was sleeping in between my car and my parents' house. In 2015, I enlisted in the military. Not long after I enlisted, I was stricken with shingles that invaded the right side of my head, very close to my eye. I temporarily lost my vision. As I endured my testing, my spiritual father, Archbishop Lorenzo Peterson, continuously spoke life into me. One of the most potent instructions he gave me was, *"Son, maintain your integrity before God."* His words of power and inspiration helped keep my mind in alignment with God's mind.

As we go through testing and persecution, we must hold fast to our faith in God. The obstacles that the Lord allows us to go through testifies that he trusts us. He believes that we will respond, react, operate, and process things his way.

When we lean and trust entirely in God, we receive the peace of God that surpasses all that we understand, and it unites our mind with his.

As believers, we must understand that God is more concerned about his glory than he is about our awards. Prioritizing God's concerns over our own sometimes requires us to willingly accept furnaces kindled with fire, dens that house lions, and crosses stained with blood. It requires us to walk in love despite the painful piercings we receive from others. When we go through levels of troubles, the writer, James, admonishes us to *"count it all joy."* (James 1:2) During the time of his writings, believers were experiencing extreme levels of persecution. Being fully aware of this, James did not adjust his instructions. James knew that believers could only remain hopeful in the midst of cruel treatment if they had the mind of Christ.

The Apostle Paul, who was no stranger to persecuting Christians or being persecuted as a Christian, teaches us in Romans 8:18 (KJV), *"For I reckon that the sufferings of this present time are not worthy to be compared with the glory which shall be revealed in us."* A far more exceeding weight of glory will come if we endure trouble with the mind of Christ. We have a hope that if we suffer with him, we will also reign with him.

"If we suffer, we shall also reign with him: if we deny him, he also will deny us."

2 Timothy 2:12 (KJV)

This hope produces joy in the face of trouble. If we learn to count our troubles joyfully and with hope, we will begin to adapt and conform to the mind of Christ.

NOTES

_____

_____

_____

_____

_____

_____

_____

_____

_____

_____

_____

_____

_____

_____

_____

_____

_____

_____

_____

_____

_____

_____

_____

it BEGINS HERE

Now that we have identified that we need the mind of Christ, our next step is to position ourselves to receive it. Our thoughts have the power to paralyze us or motivate us. They can center us in truth or lead us down a path of deception and destruction. In every moment of our lives, we are fighting an internal mental/spiritual battle that will either bring us closer to Christ or pull us further away from Him. To experience victory over the strategies of the enemy, we must obey the order of Christ. If we fail to follow the order of Christ, then we fail to submit to the thinking of Christ. Failing to submit to the thinking of Christ is embracing the thinking and philosophies of the world that holds us captive.

The Christian walk is not based on philosophies, but rather a genuine relationship with Jesus Christ where we practice thinking, behaving, and responding the way he did. Our response, behavior, and thought process must be in alignment with Christ's desires. One of the best ways to position ourselves to receive the mind of Christ is through prayer and asking God to remove all false thinking and wrong philosophies. We must ask him to align our minds with his as he grants us the power to see all things through his vision and truth.

In life, we can choose to feed our deceived, prideful, and self-destructive thinking until we become a slave to our passions, or we can focus on God's truth as he is revealed in His word. As we flood our minds with the Word of God, we will begin to conform to his image by operating in the fruit of the spirit.

"But the fruit of the Spirit is love, joy, peace, forbearance, kindness, goodness, faithfulness, gentleness and self-control."

Galatians 5:22 (NIV)

As we expel wrong thinking, we rid ourselves of impure habits. Satan wants you to believe that you are the only one who struggles and that you won't gain victory over your temptations. However, these beliefs are false. I am reminded of the old hymn that says, "What a friend we have in Jesus, all of our sins and grieves to bear, what a privilege it is to carry everything to the Lord in prayer." Christ has already made provision for our victory. We only need to choose to walk in the victory he has already given us. The choice is ours. We can choose victory by submitting to the mind of Christ or reject this victory by rejecting his mind.

In the war that we face against impure thoughts, we may lose some battles. However, the battles we lose should only increase your determination to win the war. If you expect to win the war without losing a fight, you will become discouraged very quickly. However, let us be reminded that God can redeem each defeat by revealing the root cause of our failure. If we ask, He will grant us the wisdom to get to the root of our impure thoughts and actions.

We must live out God's word until our thoughts begin to resemble his. We must be careful not to allow messages contrary to God's Word to desensitize us to God's perceptions, thoughts, reactions, actions, and attitudes. Remember, if we really want to have the mind of Christ, we must spend consistent time with Him in prayer, worship, and the meditation of his word. As we conclude this conversation, take these two truths with you and keep them in the forefront of your mind:

1. You will **never** face a temptation that is impossible to overcome.

"No temptation has overtaken you except such as is common to man; but God is faithful, who will not allow you to be tempted beyond what you are able, but with the temptation will also make the way of escape, that you may be able to bear it."

1 Corinthians 10:1 (**NIV**)

2. God is **eager** to give you all the grace you need to reject the temptation.

"Let us therefore come boldly to the throne of grace that we may obtain mercy and find grace to help in the time of need."

Hebrews 4:16 (**NKJV**)

NOTES

_____

_____

_____

_____

_____

_____

_____

_____

_____

_____

_____

_____

_____

_____

_____

_____

_____

_____

_____

_____

_____

_____

_____

_____

_____

PRAYER to UNITE our MINDS with CHRIST

Dear Father,

In the name of Jesus Christ our Lord, I pray that you have your way in our lives. Thank you for your power, goodness, mercy, and everlasting love.

Wash us with your precious blood, and cleanse us from all impurities, in the name of Jesus Christ. Wash and submerge our minds in your blood. Forgive us of any offenses that we may have committed against you, knowingly and unknowingly. If we have opened any doors, spiritually or naturally, that are unpleasing unto you, we ask that you shut them.

Clear our minds of any preconceived thoughts, confusion, or deception. As we lay down our will and pick up your will, give us clear minds. Clarify our vision and thoughts, give us wisdom, correct our actions, and reactions, and obliterate any sinful habits. Block anything that is not of you that we may hear Your Voice clearer than any other. Restore the years in which we were complacent in sinful thinking.

We vow to glorify you for who you are and the things you have done.

There is none like you, and we submit our bodies and minds to be used by you. Father, thank you for your wisdom. Thank you for your goodness, mercy, and love. We love you, and we will obey.

Amen!

author
ACKNOWLEDGMENTS

There are so many individuals who played a part in my journey to becoming a published author. Whether you encouraged me to keep pushing in a difficult season of my life, or inspired me from a distance: *Thank you!*

To my family, my mother, father, and brother, thank you for your support. I am so grateful. I love each of you. To my spiritual father, Archbishop Lorenzo N. Peterson, thank you for your leadership, mentorship, guidance, patience, and love. I love you dearly. To Apostle Gerald Flint, thank you for your inspiration, guidance, and tough love. I love you.

To you, my amazing reader, thank you for supporting my freshman book. I pray that it is a blessing to your life and that you will share this message with others.

meet the
AUTHOR

Author Michael Roberson is a proud native of Raleigh, North Carolina. He is a devoted father, and proud soldier of the US Army. Michael is a dedicated student of the Gospel and continues to seek the Kingdom of God through every area of his life.

As an ordained minister of the Gospel, Michael is enthusiastic about sharing his love for God and discipling others on their walk with Christ. It was this passion that inspired him to write his first book, The Mind of Christ. This impactful read was designed to help Christians experience the true fruit of Jesus Christ by surrendering to Christ's instructions for our lives. As you read this book, you will be challenged to take a closer look at your daily productivity, the thoughts you dwell on, and what you believe about Jesus Christ.

In 2010, Michael acknowledged and accepted his call into ministry and began teaching the word of God at New

Hope Freedom and Deliverance Cathedral of Louisburg, NC, under the leadership of Dr. Lorenzo N. Peterson, the Presiding Prelate of the International Ministers Covenant Fellowship and International Apostolic Communion. He was licensed as a Minister in 2015, and later ordained as a reverend. He received his Bachelor's degree in Theological Studies 2017 and his Master's degree in Theological Studies 2020 from Regency Christian College of Jacksonville Florida. His source of courage and strength can be found in one of his favorite scriptures, 1 Thessalonians 5:18, "In everything give thanks; for this is the will of God in Christ Jesus concerning you." This scripture also reminds Michael that no matter the plans that are set within a man's heart, the Lord's Word will prevail.

Michael joined the United States Army in March 2015. After serving three years in the military at Fort Wainwright, Alaska he later moved to Huntsville, Alabama and then Baton Rouge, Louisiana.

When he's not teaching or sharing Christ, Michael enjoys sports, traveling the world, experiencing different culture, stay up to date on all the latest fashions, trying new foods, and checking out new movie releases.

stay CONNECTED

Thank you for reading, *the MIND of CHRIST: Impacting Lives, Transforming Minds.* Michael looks forward to connecting with you. Here are a few ways you can connect with the author and stay updated on new releases, speaking engagements, products, and more.

FACEBOOK   MICHAEL A. ROBERSON, Jr.
INSTAGRAM   @michaelarobersonjr
WEBSITE   www.michaelarobersonjr.com
EMAIL   mrobers2.yeshua@yahoo.com

Made in the USA
Columbia, SC
17 March 2021

33993741R00052